Thank you to the Banta Brigade, the TWP, Seb Forest and 108 Tattoo Shop, what remains of the Blue Moon Crew, everyone at the Pole Hill Camp, Nouveau Bleach, Loz Vegas, London Poetry Books, Alfie, PISSKRIEG, Tolly, Paul, Saul and everyone else who has tolerated Redeeming Features.

redeemingfeaturespoetry@yahoo.com

@redeemingf

Cover artwork by Seb Forest of 108 Tattoo Shop

In memory of my Mum.

Contents

Horse Box Orgies

Don't attend Horse Box Orgies, it's never going to end well
You'll find yourself trapped inside a horse box orgy hell
3.5 tons of vehicle shaking
There's banging and crashing inside
It all seems like fun and games until you have to swallow your pride
Orgies in a horse box? Way too tighter space
There's barely room to work out what's an arse and what's a face

Horse Box Orgies are a disaster waiting to occur
The writhing mass of perspiration will all start to blur
Forget about Horse Box Orgies, you'll share everything that's yours
If one of you has the clap you'll all end up with a round of applause
If you receive an invite to a Horse Box Orgy just say nay
Even if you manage to have a good time, your sexual health may pay
Only fools and horses, only disappointment and shame
Horse box orgies are a fucking shit show, the idea is insane

Farmyard vehicle sex parties should only be for horses
It won't strengthen your relationship they just end in divorces
Horse Box Orgies are a bad idea, they descend into violence
All the elation and merriment can swiftly turn to silence
To hell with Horse Box Orgies, it'll always end in tears
It kicks off more at Horse Box Orgies than you've seen in years
Horse Box sex parties cause mayhem, you'd never believe what I saw
There's more drama at Horse Box Orgies than on Channel Four

Do not frequent Horse Box Orgies they're a terrible idea

When people mention them to me I get the Horse Box fear
If you get summoned to a Horse Box Orgy you should always negate
Equestrian transportation vehicles are no place to fornicate
Who's bright idea were Horse Box Orgies? Who thought of this awful game?
Find another venue, and save yourself the pain

Flat Feet

When I was a kid people noticed that I walked crooked
Then they took a closer look, they found I was flat footed
Your feet are far too flat they said, you'll never pass a medical
Your feet are the wrong shape they said, they need to be more spherical
Your feet need to be tough they said, your feet should have a curve
Your feet look fucking rough they said, no purpose will they serve
Your feet are like sheets of A4, your feet are pancake flat
Your feet are the flattest I've ever seen before, your feet are like an old man's hat
Your foot looks like a broken branch, it needs a Doctor's view
When I see what hangs off your legs it makes me want to spew
Your feet are bloody terrifying, your feet give me a fright
Your feet remind me of Frankenstein, they keep me up at night
Your trotters are in a state they said, your arches should swerve like a disk
Your feet look like roadkill they said, your feet are on the piss
Your feet look like they're trapped beneath a huge enormous weight
Your feet should have a bend they said, your feet are flat like a plate
You're a Chiropodist's worst enemy, a Podiatry nightmare
Your feet have all gone wrong they said, your feet give me a scare
Your feet are tone deaf, out of key, your feet are note imperfect
Your feet are starting to trouble me, your feet ain't even worth it
I learned to live with my out of shape, warped, bent and deformed bone
My knees would bang together, as I hobbled my way home

Bus Lane Payments

Bus lane payments
In the mail
A terrible crime, beyond the pale
The price I pay, my repentance
35 quid is my sentence

Bus lane payments
Essex towns
Causing grief and rage and frowns
Bus lane payments not again
Bus lane now and bus lane then
I can't seem to stay within
The lanes that drivers are given

Bus lane payments
Through the post
Disappearing, going ghost
Not again, what a pain
Paying to drive in the bus lane

Bus lane payments
On the run
Paying for the bus lane is no fun
Avoiding the authorities
Misplacing my priorities

Bus lane, bus lane keep your head down
Bus lane, Bus lane skipping town
Bus lane payments. Groundhog day.

When there's traffic the bus lane is the only way
Even if you're in receipt of benefits. Claimant.
In debt and missing your repayment
No point in appealing becoming a complainant
I fucking hate bus lane payments

Explosive Diarrhoea

Diarrhoea
Loud and clear
Live in fear
Ignition near
Terrified and knowing
Of the constant flowing
Like a waterfall
A gift from nature, or manmade. Wier.
Oops, oh deer
Asshole burning
Like Brighton pier
Shed a tear
Exhausted
Losing power
Like King Lear

Way too runny
Not so funny
Bowl atrocity
Fine viscosity
Give in. Come what may.
Faecal eruption like Pompeii
Food poisoning, die another day
Like James bond
Putrid brown pond
Quaking, Shaken and stirred
Living in constant fear of the turd
Bog brush toil
Casino Royal
Not going to make it. Cubicle scramble.

Gamble
Texas Holdem
Sweat turns cold n'
Legs are folding
Touching cloth
Feel
The broken the seal
Yesterday's meal
Deal
With your hand, keep it in
Play your cards right
Try and win
Clench your hole tight
Delirious rooms that spin
Shit smeared arms
Poo Stained palms
F1 speed, obscene
Latrine-pit stop.
Please stop!
Lesson learned like Aesop's
Fable
Stool on both the floor and the table
Cause a mess and then abscond
There's no magic wand
Harry Plopta'
I forgot the
Secret spell
To escape from this hell
There's no way out
Detox, shit out the gout
Evasive manoeuvres
Ice cube soothers

Discharge oozes
Hear nothing, see nothing, errrrgh chuffing
The nightmare continues
Grab the bin use
Anything that is to hand
Referencing bowl conditions and a hardcore band
Look at the poo it's barely solid
Liquid, not moulded

Harsh words
Arses firing out turds
With enough power to score goals
Like Paul Scholes
Red holes
Angry souls
Death toll
Don't catch it
Sachet
Movicol
Yellow and brown
Trickling down
Inside my thigh
Oh please why
Don't get in my eye
Ammonia
The world over
Cardiff to Catalonia
The arse excretes
The shit defeats
And stains the sheets
Makes us Melancholy like Keats
Arseholes spurting like toilet teats

Everyone gets it, Bankers and NEETS
Unwanted intrusions from your rear
The curse of explosive Diarrhoea.

Job and Knock

Job and Knock
Watching the clock
Keeping stock
Of the time we've got

Friday brings us a rare gift
You still get paid but don't finish your shift
The boss has got a place to be
But he'll still pay us currency

If we finish before the end of the day
And the job's done then we'll still earn our pay
Working quick-smart, finger to bone
In a couple of hours we're going home

Job and Knock, team work's what you need
Grafting like you're buzzing on speed
Don't eat lunch, save your grub
Soon enough we'll be down the pub

Don't stop to smoke, don't stop for tea
Its Job and Knock, its A to B
Pushing your ability
To exit the facility

Job and Knock, going home
Job and Knock then free to roam
Job and Knock, earn your cash
Job and Knock then off we dash

We don't falter, we don't stop
Not today, its Job and Knock
Up and down knees like springs
Lets see what the weekend brings

Put your tools down, stop looking surly
Its 4pm, we're leaving early
We're Job N' knocking', it's our turn
Me, the boss and the whole firm

Job and Knock, out we go
Job and Knock, we all know
You get the job done then you stop
The weekend's here, its Job and Knock

Riot At The Yoga Retreat

Riot at the yoga retreat
The hippies took a stand
Acts of civil disobedience
That certainly weren't planned

It kicked off at the yoga retreat
In the lotus they all sat
Who would've thought?
Despite what they were taught
They swapped the yoga mat
For a baseball bat

The yoga retreat was meant to be
A weekend of tranquil reflection
And silence, but the hippies had enough of it
And they all resorted to violence

What happened to the cat pose?
What about the frog?
And the downward facing dog?
Before we knew it
There were riot police
Emerging from the fog

Chaos at the yoga retreat
There were sandals everywhere
We all asked the hippies to calm it down
But they didn't fucking care

It spilled out
From the studio onto the street
The Dalai Lama was there
For a meet and greet,
Despite the tear gas
The hippies wouldn't admit defeat.

RIOT AT THE YOGA RETREAT!!!!!

Dogging DJ Wez

His name is dogging DJ Wez
He's never been dogging he says
He'll deny it till he's blue in the face
But he goes dogging all-round the place

A marauder of the car park scene
You should see a list of the places he's been
Notches scratched on the bodywork keep the score
His life is a constant dogging tour

His seconded favourite pastime is
Playing records to the kids
But when Wez's DJ set is done
He's off to have some dogging fun

More roadside sessions than you've had hot dinners
An entourage of rabbit masked sinners
Wink, nudge, he tells you it ain't the truth
But Wez knows that we all have proof

He gives interviews to the press
You want to know more but he'll make you guess
He keeps an air of mystery
That's the magic of dogging you see

Late night hero, backstreet voyeur
Indecent exposure-paranoia
Body fluid on the back of the Chevy
His dogging prowess is somewhat heavy

His name ain't Mark,
It ain't Steve,
It ain't Bez,
His name is dogging DJ Wez.

Bed Bugs

Bugs that live inside your bed
Bugs that crawl around your head
You wish the fucking bugs were dead!

Bugs that leave you seeing red
Like 'Minor Threat',
The bug's debt
Is the sleep they took
Just like a crook,

Tried to read your book
Then you took a look
Down, and the bugs left you shook
Like Captain Hook.

Bad life plan like Peter Pan, skull rock
Blowing up, ticking clock
All over my back and tail-bone-gator
I hope I don't see the bugs later
Hemiptera. Anger-generator
In a while crocodile
Bugs put your temper on trial
Raging, turning up the dial

Bugs that live inside your bed
Bugs that leave you filled with dread
I'd rather sleep out in the shed,
Pain worse than a broken leg
Doctor! Dose me up with medical grade
Downers. Nodding off. Danger,

Waxy candle holder, like Slade
Benzo eases the bugs tickle,

Fleeting fickle
Bed fellow
Puke that's yellow.
Life was mellow
Then, oh hello
Uninvited
I was benighted
Now I see the light
It got switched on
When I started screaming
Bugs interrupted my lucid dreaming
Not a wet one, no unconscious creaming.

No! I did not awake beaming
It doesn't rain its fucking teeming

This will take hours and days of cleaning
Not to leave the place shiny and gleaming;
But irradiation from red hot steaming
Driven insane by pesky bed Bugs
Causing Madness, as if their name is Suggs.

You're the food the Bugs were fed
Bugs that make you wished you'd fled
Pissed off. Red line, like a stolen ped.
Bugs that live inside your bed.

Skinhead Dave

There's a gentlemen in a seaside town
You can't tell when he wears a frown
Because he shaves off every inch of his hair
Passersby all stop and stare

Even his eyebrows get the razor
He's a scary bloke but don't let it phase ya'
Crombie, DMs, Levi Jeans
Tightly turned up at the seams
At a young age he shaved off his mane
Skinhead Dave is his name

But the funny thing about this fella
With his cold bald head out whatever the weather
Is you'd never guess what his job is
His mates can't help but take the piss
Every morning rain or shine
He's there on the production line

Bottling up
Couldn't give a fuck
A thousand shiny bottles all in a row
The benefits of them he'll never know
What a way to spend his time
Grafting, thinking "these will never be mine"

Despite his total lack of hair
Skinhead Dave works in a shampoo factory I swear

Worms

Heinous painus
Deep within the anus
Talking Frank like Shameless
The Doctor tried to blame us

Aimless
Nameless
Worms that invade us
The gift the dirt gave us
People try and shame us

You wouldn't want to be me
Mate you should have seen me
Scratchy in betweeny
These wriggles are keeny
Fever nightmare. Dreamy.

Tiny little movers
Titchy
Scratchy manoeuvres
Itchy
It feels like I've got a stitchy

Obscene poetry
Not like Yeats or Heaney
Seamus
No I wasn't blameless

I'm appalling
Lacking decorum

Many tried to tame
But to no gain
They tell me to learn manners
Like, Judy Dench the Dame
'Sort yourself out, Redeeming', they say
But I wouldn't have it any other way

Worms
Worms
Caused by germs
The germs cause worms
And the worms take turns
To cause gurns
It burns
And the worms take pride
And reside inside us on their own terms
WORMS!!

Save It For the Dojo

Cocaine, steroids and heartbreak. Oh no
Soaring heights make you reach new lows, bro.
Mad. Jumping around like a march hare. Pogo.
Driven away in a meat-wagon, solo.
Blood stains all down a 50 quid polo
Too much pride. Walking away was a no-go.

Caught in the moment
Regretful morning, craving atonement
Thinking you are as 'ard as
Bruce Lee, Ali and Diaz
Red faced raging, eclipsed pupils, purple vein eyes
Like Nate, no one was surprised
When even if you win, you admit defeat
Sprawled out, apprehended in the street

No one cares that you proved you're tough
When your wrist is locked into a hand cuff
The lonely nights-in start to drag
When your ankle is bound by a tag

But what a sad terrible show though
All to conquer a 5 minute foe
Your anger had to go somewhere so
Next time save it for the dojo

The Haunted Garden of Hither Green

I'm going to tell you a tale of evil and witchcraft, cruel and mean

It was the year of 2015
You'd never believe the things we've seen
In the haunted Garden of Hither Green
The profession of landscaping
Became psychology breaking
As a women of the black magic kind
Used sorcery to control the mind

You'd find your sanity would unwind
Your brain would feel empty and you'd go blind
The sights our eyes fell upon were obscene
In the haunted Garden of Hither Green
The drinks she gave us made us feel lean
The curse took over the whole team
Objects appeared before our eyes
I bet you think I'm telling lies

The hellish images could never have been
Foretold or indeed foreseen
In the haunted Garden of Hither Green
Apparitions from your darkest dream
Her looks made people fall down the stairs
I've never seen such menacing glares
She'd peer down and clearly not care
One guy fell flat on his face and was made aware
Of the magic that was at play
A new incident would occur each day

People refused to work there
None of them would even dare
Enter into the witch's lair
We were under the spell of an evil queen
In the Haunted Garden of Hither Green
A priest would call the place spiritually unclean
Our colleagues absented, they weren't keen
I trembled in my oesophagus, my abdomen and my spleen

Not purgatory or hell, somewhere in between
The poisoned drinks and broth would make us sick
Some kind of twisted magic trick
Nothing we built would ever stay level
The work of an old school South London Devil
Our infected work force's complexion
Had a pale white sheen
In the Haunted Garden of Hither Green
Nothing grew, only our vomit was green
She poisoned the soup, the tea and the tagine

No one else would show up to work
But me and my mate Saul would never shirk
Even though it meant that we got cursed
The Garden had already put us through the worst
Everything seemed to have an earie gleam
In the Haunted Garden of Hither Green
It felt like every day was Halloween
We went to dark places that we'd never been

It turns out nearby was some children's mass grave
That tragically no-one could save
A train crash that left many dead, though the details were vague

As well as burial pits from the Plague
The cold biting winds made life far from serene
In the haunted Garden of Hither Green
We liaised with the dead in our daily routine
A clairvoyant would've wanted to intervene

Still we never succumbed to defeat
Even though each dark day felt stuck on repeat
It took a ten day silent meditation retreat
For some of us to get back on our feet
And I can tell you to this day
There is a word that those who worked there still never say
We dare not utter the client's name, like Macbeth
For fear of the curse bringing us an early death

Throughout the job our nights were filled with an unsettling dream
This seemed to come from the enchanted cuisine
She spiked the water, the milk and the caffeine
Cursed stew made with veg, poison and bean
It was like a visit to hell's canteen
I'll be honest though I've never even tried a tagine
It was at about when I was writing line 18
That I realised a shit ton of words rhyme with Green
But believe me and you
The rest is all true
I longed to plan a great escape
Get far away from there, perhaps emigrate
Incarcerated in this macabre garden, it was a terrible scene
I wanted to jump the fence like Steve Mcqueen
Working late on a damp cold night like Avril Lavine
I don't know what it was all supposed to mean
But these morbid visions can never be unseen

With that witch of black magic, I hope I never reconvene
In the Haunted Garden of Hither Green

Indoor Rock Climbing and Super-Heroes

Spiderman came to the climbing wall. He made us all look like mugs

If I didn't know he had superpowers, I'd think he was on drugs

Spiderman arrived at the climbing gym, he whizzed up and down the wall

He walked up it like it wasn't vertical and there was no wall there at all

Spiderman appeared at the climbing centre, he started to scale the ceiling

He achieved anti-gravity feats that I never would've believed in

Spiderman turned up to have a climb and left the place covered in web

The arachnid Homosapien, nature's cross species celeb

He ran up then down and didn't fall
He may as well have been 10 foot tall
He scaled the place with no trouble at all
Spiderman came to the climbing wall

Raving Bebhinn

(N.B The correct pronunciation of the Irish name Bebhinn is Baven)

Raving Bebhinn
The night she's savin'
It was going to be a quiet one, but now we're all caving

Up to the usual miss-behaving
We're leaving on a jet plane n'
Never coming back again

In the Arctic like Shackleton or the Alps like Hannibal
International party animal
Not an alien or a cannibal

Going off like compressed propane. Flammable.
The party only starts when she kicks the door in
A powerhouse of debaucherous sin

Intrepid 7 day bender,
Shindig explorer
Compared to her your parties are poorer

This poem can only give you a flavour
Of the phenomenon that is
Bebhinn the raver

Beware of the contraband that she gave ya'
The double pill, no sleep till, anti-buzz kill party savour

Summer fields or cold winter braving
It's always more that she leaves the revellers craving
In on the tiles or out on the paving
Brace yourself, I doubt you're ready for raving Bebhinn

Haircut

Locks
Lots of locks
Lots of ginger locks
Locks of ginger hair
Spilling over a denim jacket
Covered in pins and patches
They didn't appreciate it at football matches

I was kicked out of school, for being a fool
Too fool for school
And I had a girlfriend you see
She was older than me
I thought she was the business
But the problem was
She only liked me for my hair
I swear
The only reason she was there
Was my hair

In Brighton I got befriended by a gang of skinheads
They got me to shave my head
Be one of the boys they said
All well and good down the pub
But back at home, one day she turned up
At my door
She couldn't believe what she saw
It was gone, my hair
She loved my hair
The only reason we were a pair

Was my hair
I swear
It was gone
I'd caught her unaware

"What is that?" she said
"It's my head"
I said "My hair's still red'
Then she fled
We were never to be wed
What had I done
This was no fun
12 years old
I'd gone bald
Lost my girl
My minds in a swirl
The cheek
She only wanted me coz I was a freak
Without a care
And long hair
Patches and stud
Now I looked like a thug
She only loved me for my hair
She just wanted the follicles
Not the other molecules
That make up me
Shallow
The hair cut set me free
She went off and let me be

Not long after
She was at the door

Now she'd changed the score
She wanted me back
Imagine the cheek of that
Oh dear
Too late
I don't care
She only wanted me for my hair

Amber Gambler

Foot down, floor it
In your ears, can't ignore it
Cruise it, spin it, tour it
Handbrake turn, you should have sawn it

Orange flash
And off he dash
One step down from red for a second
The calling of the throttle beckoned

North of the river
In a rush and a diver
Induction, compression, ignition, exhaust
A gambler's luck has run its course

Swerving bikes, a head on crash
Pissed off horn be-be-beep bash
If he didn't stop then he won't stop now
Head on collision, windscreen, POW!!

You hear him coming like a drum band. Samba.
King of the road, crown, like bowed timber. Camber.
Like Northern Soul, accelerated Motown. Tamla.
Red lining and venting anger
Mind out of the way for the amber gambler

Line Crossing

Who went and brought up the great Tabu?
Who had to have their say?
Someone spoke of it in the toilet queue
They'll be kicked out and sent on their way
Who was the cunt
Who exhaled this affront
Was it sincere or was it a stunt
The public should apprehend this punk
Unfortunately the rumours are all true
Someone brought up the great Tabu

Was it you that mentioned the great Tabu?
Or was it one of your mates?
When you rap your lips round this subject
People hate the sound that it makes
What demon creatures
With no Redeeming Features
Some gang of vermin, a posse of leeches
A satanic cabal of evil preachers
Like eating raw lemons not apples or peaches
They're more Nihilistic than Nietzsche's teachers
Who brought up the great Tabu?

Someone shouted the great Tabu
Here we go again
I hope they'll stop, but are they going to?
They've been at it since God knows when
Which individuals
Painted these visuals
Clearly in my mind

The images in front of my eyes
Make me wish that I was blind
What gang of dicks ?
What bunch of pricks?
What unorthodox
Motley Crew of cocks?
It wasn't me and it wasn't you
Who brought up the great Tabu?
Who was it who raised the great Tabu?
That was over the line
They dared utter these words to you
They've really done it this time
Some arsehole army
Driving me barmy
With their inappropriate
(Someone pass the opiate)
Sick use of the verbal
I need some herbal
Remedy from this sickening feeling
Who's holding? Who's dealing?
5 or 4 or 3 or 2
One too many times that's all I knew
I can't think what I should do
Who brought up the great Tabu

Which man went and verbalised this obvious no-go zone?
He must have acted as part of a clique, he can't have done it alone
A group of undesirables
At least they are reliables
They always give you a guarantee
To find a way to piss off you and me
They've started a row

This needs dropping now
Like tin foil it's hard to swallow and chew
Like your enemy standing next to you
The damage is too much to undo
Who brought up the great Tabu?

Which bright spark started arguing
And ideologically bargaining?
Which genius thought this plan was great
And initiated this endless debate?
Their audacity makes me feel irate
Words too foul to imitate
This is enough on everyone's plate
Stuck between a cunt and an angry face
A knuckle-duster and a can of mace
A losing battle and last place in a race
A politico and a hard-case
I'm sick to death of this audible spew
Who brought up the great Tabu?

Who are this crowd of proud provocateurs ?
God of war, Mars in furs
Blimey, shiny whips of displeasure
It wasn't time to drop the Tabu bomb, then or never
In retrospect it wasn't clever
I was just waiting in line for the loo
Who brought up the great Tabu?

Some blokes vomited up the great Tabu
It was always going to be the men
They like saying things to shock and upset you
When they've had a beer now and then

I've gotta go
Does anyone know?
Just who they are?
Did they travel far?
By train bus or car?
Which one abruptly started it?
Spat, shat out and farted it
The obnoxious picture that they drew
They said it right in front of you
I need a shit so I can't walk away
With my bleeding ears I'll have to pay
Locking us up here in their Tabu cell
It makes me feel grim and unwell
It's Tabu can't you tell?
I'll talk Tabu with you in hell

Now the foot is on the other shoe
You don't like it when it's done to you
Light bulb moment
Too late for atonement
Now the roles are reversed
Things start to get even worse
As the offended becomes the offender
And the defensive refuse to surrender
The one thing that they shouldn't say
Is the only way
To get their payback
By continuing the never ending
Offending
Not liking the taste of their own medicine
Electric culture shock like Edison
Now this cunt gang's eyes are raging

40

Their booze red skin is rapidly ageing
Mortal Combat mind state, no rules to engaging
You shouldn't have said
Now they've all seen red
Not enjoying it when it's done to you
That's what you get for spoiling the view
They won't enjoy hearing it but it's true
Now someone's brought up their great Tabu

Shady Characters

Wearing sunglasses indoors
Watching Brit Cops or doing chores
The shadiest, edgiest novelty
That no one except you can see

Wearing sunglasses indoors
Hoover the carpet, scrub the floors
Who cares if its Sunday morning
The rent is due and the landlord's storming

Wearing sunglasses after dark
Hallucinogenic manoeuvres in the park
I can't moonwalk and I can't jive
But the shades make me feel like M15

Standing inside wearing shades
Air guitar, Bomber ace of spades
What the indoor eye protection is for
Is simulating a world tour

Wearing sunglasses in your home
Playing Wembley all alone
Doing interviews down the phone
The Job Centre feels like the 'Rolling Stone'

3 day bender, 3 days lost
Ignore the brain fry, disregard the cost
None of that matters when you look the bizz
5 quid pasty base off white wizz

It ain't for a purpose, ain't for a cause
Back stage behind homeless hostel doors
Let's give ourselves a round of applause
For wearing sunglasses indoors

The Planet of the Scaffolders

They blast out one arm bench presses and shot-put giant boulders
On the planet of the Scaffolders
They'll crush you with their forearm strength
Wielding poles of enormous length
Biceps like Saturn's Titan-moon
If they're after you they'll find you soon
Their thumbs are as big as a serving spoon
As you and I grow these beasts never get older
On the Planet of the Scaffolder

Booming voices
And early 2000s tattoo choices
Their calves are the size of an ancient tree
With super speed hypertrophy
They'll climb up and down your house
Compared to them you look like a mouse
Body temperature hotter than a stocked up sauna
Through snow and ice they never get colder
On the Planet of the Scaffolder
Silver backs
Narrowly avoiding over exertion induced heart attacks
Stomping along steel frame scaffolding
Strongest man record holding
Radio playing
40 Stone weighing
Music blaring
Flexing and raring
You can't see past their humongous shoulders
On the Planet of the Scaffolders

P.C. Smith

There's a fearsome man in my home town
A man who enforces the law
A man who strikes fear into you when he knocks at your door
His name is not Columbo, Morse, Lewis or Shaft
He makes them all look like amateurs, he's a master of his craft
This man is the stuff of folklore, a legend and a myth

He lurks beneath the hedgerows
And his name is P.C. Smith

P.C. Smith hunts down criminals twenty four hours a day
P.C. Smith will catch you if you try and run away
P.C. Smith is always ten steps ahead of you
P.C. Smith will arrest you and he'll nick all your mates too
P.C. Smith is strong and fast and he's coming after you

(With his reputation you'd think he's related to Will from Bad Boys 2
He works for MI5, the CIA and the KGB)

P.C. Smith is far beyond the Bobby that we all see
P.C. Smith has eyes and ears in places we don't know
P.C. Smith should be given his own prime-time cop show……..
P.C. Smith mainly hates teenagers smoking weed
P.C. Smith always appears from where he can't be seen
(He hides in the bushes pouncing on stoners all the time)

P.C. Smith hates smoking weed, he thinks it's a heinous crime
If you're smoking a joint within a mile radius of him
He'll sniff you out and book you as soon as he can

You cannot get away from him, no matter what your plan
If P.C. Smith is on your case you best find a good lawyer
So if he appears out of the blue, don't say I didn't warn ya'

Coronation

The audience participation
And idol worship abomination
Gave me a sickening sensation
My stomach needed examination.

'You guessed it'. I wasn't viewing
To avoid projectile spewing
They still thought their blood was blue
Way back in 1952.
It seems today they still do too
They think they're better than me and you.

Imperial Nostalgia Masturbation,
Captivated population,
Feudal fantasy simulation,
Constant newsfeed, over stimulation,
Unnecessary adulation;
There was a coronation-quiche
To help us get though
At least they did something for me and you.
Out of the goodness of their heart
Add the ingredients to your shopping cart.

Pledge allegiance
Allegiance to who?
Pledge allegiance, allegiance to you?
You thought that's what we were going to do?
Who the flying fuck are you?
Pledge allegiance, drink to your health

Sing your praises, speak for yourself;
Avoiding the hype, ignoring the media storm, head down. Stealth.
Pledge allegiance? Fuck yourself.

No wonder there was a demonstration
Foreseen predicted tribulation
Unleashing pent up frustration
There's no need for deliberation
To hell with Charlie's Coronation.

Portaloo

One morning we got a delivery at work, of the lavatory kind
With a bemusing sign attached to it, that confused my mind
The sign read "7 Capacity Portaloo"
7 folks inside
They said you could fit 7 guys in here
But the Portaloo lied

6 plus 1 in a Portaloo
5 and 2 in a box
Too much shit in a Portaloo,
You could catch the Portaloo pox
Disease spreads in overcrowded Portaloos
Packed Portaloos make you ill
Believe me above capacity Portaloos
Can maim and they can kill

It's a challenge to even get 4 humans through the entrance
Trying to fit a load of people in a Portaloo is a joke
And a stool soaked death sentence
4 then 5 then 6 then 7
We'll die and go to Portaloo heaven

7 dead in a Portaloo, that's what the headlines will tell
Too many heads in a Portaloo and we're all going straight to hell
Site meetings inside a Portaloo are certainly a hard sell
These excrement filled Tardis defaecation stations can make you unwell
I thought that it was obvious but in case you can't tell
7 inside one Portaloo is too many personnel

Evacuate and slam the door

This ain't what I came to work for
All aboard the blue box shit pile party
It's bacteria ridden so I hope you're feeling hardy

Portaloo, Portaloo one at a time
The death box noxious faeces shrine
But then we soon realised that all was not what it seems
7 people could shit in there before it gets drained
That's what the sign means
Trying to get 2 in a Portaloo? Split that straight in half
7 people to a Portaloo? You must be having a laugh

I'd rather be a bum than an arsehole

I'd rather be a bum than an arsehole
Work place aggro can take its toll
Boss man, lost man, we all pay the cost man
Ice cold man like Jack frost with a business plan

I'd rather live in chaos than need control
I'd rather sell pills than sell my soul
I'd rather be a scrounger than a thief
I'd sooner have no teeth than deal with the beef

Work place. Time waste.
Unmet needs leaves sour taste
Running out of toothpaste
Get that angry look off of your face

Gratitude, not attitude
I need the doe
I've got nowhere to go
And nothing to show
But I'll let you know
That I'm done
And off I run

Because the boss don't care
About you so be aware
Never trust the hand that bleeds you
Prioritize the ones who need you

People judge you for claiming the dole
Mark my words, record it, let the cameras roll

Don't let your job leave you in bottomless hole
I'd rather be a bum than an arsehole

Sniffing Glue and Playing Chicken on the M4

Sniffing glue and playing chicken on the M4
Acts of insanity like you've never seen before
Our hero is a sticky character with something up his sleeve
Avoiding vehicles at speeds that you wouldn't believe

Abusing aerosols and dodging traffic on the M5
It's a wonder how he's still alive
His deodorant can make him smell great
But his brain has begun to disintegrate

Huffing Tipex and running in front of vans on the M32
This one's for the Bristol hippy crew
His bravery makes him look 'ard to his mates
But if he gets hit, that Tipex can't correct his mistakes

Shoving marker pens up your nose
And jumping around in the fast lane
During rush hour on the M11
Thrill seeking and a one-way ticket to heaven
The buzz leaves our hero craving more
Sniffing glue and playing chicken on the M4

Other excellent titles from London Poetry Books

There is a Tune.	*Cathy Flower*
Dark Matter.	*Amy Smith*
Pathways.	*Anne Gaelan*
The Mirrors of Thespis	
Pocket full of Whispers.	
Kiss of the Honey Bees.	*Keith Robert Bray*
Counteroffensive.	*Steve Tasane*
English is a Foreign,	
Language.	
Outside in musin on life as an,	
Autistic Poet.	*Alain English*
Ooetry.	*Wendy Young*
Death Suicide Despair Poetry.	
Life and Hope.	*Jason Harris*
In the Name of the Flesh.	*Ernesto Sarezale*
The Bird of Morning	
Of the deep.	*IDF. Andrew*
Twisted and Chewed 2.	*Shaun Rivers*
Tomorrow We Fight,	
Yesterday's Men.	*Lizzie Rose*
Everybody is a diagnosis.	*Richard Allan*
Running Through Trees,	
And Glitter.	*Rachel Tansy Chadwick*
My Inside Opened Out	*Patricia Flowers*

Printed and bound by CPI Group (UK) Ltd, Croydon, CR0 4YY

09/04/2024

03768405-0001